Beading with Herringbone Stitch

BEADING WITH
HERRINGBONE
STITCH

A BEADWORK HOW-TO BOOK

VICKI STAR

INTERWEAVE PRESS

Editor, Jean Campbell
Copy editor, Stephen Beal
Proofreader, Nancy Arndt
Illustration, Gayle Ford
Photography, except where noted, Joe Coca
Design and production, Dean Howes
Cover design, Bren Frisch
Print management, Don Schmidt

Beadwork Magazine
Interweave Press
201 East Fourth Street
Loveland, Colorado 80537-5655 USA
www.interweave.com

Printed in Canada

Library of Congress Cataloging-in-Publication Data

Star, Vicki, 1955–
    Beading with herringbone stitch / Vicki Star.
        p. cm. — (A beadwork how-to-book)
    Includes bibliographical references and index.
    ISBN 1-883010-99-3
        1. Beadwork I. Beadwork (Loveland, Colo.) II. Title. III. Series.

TT860 .S737 2001
745.58'2—dc21   2001039267

First printing: IWP-10M:901:FR

DEDICATION

This book is dedicated to Moms and Grandmoms everywhere,

especially my own Mom and Grandma,

who always encouraged and nurtured my creativity.

Acknowledgements

I'd like to acknowledge Stephney Hornblow and
the Bead Ladies at Mimotla and Botshebelo.
Thank you so much for sharing.
And thanks to everyone who took the time to send
photos and beadwork to me.

CONTENTS

INTRODUCTION

If you've been beading for any length of time, you'll know what I mean when I say that beading evolves. I'm constantly discovering new tools, new techniques, and new BEADS!

Students and other beady-eyed friends bring new goodies to class, or I'll see a new color or bead shape in a favorite bead store, or I'll come across a new book with a technique or variation different from any I've seen before. These discoveries are a part of what keeps me interested in beadwork. The other part is the actual physical creative process—the beads and the beading!

I've always had a really hard time making more than one of the same thing. The second earring is a real challenge (I've got lots of singles lying about). Same with stitches: Once I've figured out how to do a stitch, I want to try the next thing, or make it with a different bead or pattern. "What if you go through the beads THIS way instead of THAT way?" I ask myself. I really want to invent a new stitch, but each time I think I've succeeded, I'll see it in a book or magazine within a few days. Weird how the cosmos works!

I also have a drawer full of what I call false starts—beadwork that didn't go quite the way I wanted. I always learn from these false starts, because something different can lead to the way that works for me, and give the result I was looking for.

In this book, I share with you my explorations in herringbone stitch. I wish the book contained every technique and variation that uses this stitch, but I know that's just not possible. There will always be someone, somewhere, who does it just a little bit different or takes it in a new direction.

So, settle down and enjoy! I hope that this book gives you a solid foundation in herringbone stitch and inspires you to invent your own variations.

Happy Beading!
Vicki Star

HISTORY

Herringbone stitch has recently become popular in the United States through its use by the Ndebele (pronounced en-duh-BELL-y or en-DE-bull-lee) of South Africa. These people are descendants of the Nguni Tribe and live mostly in the Pretoria and Mpumalanga areas of South Africa. They have their own language called si-Ndebele.

As a result of their powerful warring history, the Ndebele have always managed to keep a strong tribal identity, in spite of the influences of the cultures they have conquered as well as those to whom they have lost. Find out more about their military history at right.

Beaders at Mimotla.

Photo by Stephney Hornblow

Pietersburg

Pretoria ★

SWAZILAND

• Welkom
Kimberley
Bloemfontein ★   LESOTHO
De Aar   • Durban

SOUTH AFRICA   Umtata

• Beaufort West

East London
• Oudtshoorn
Cape Town ★   Port Elizabeth

NDEBELE TRIBAL HISTORY

Early 1800s: Rise of tribal leader Mzilikazi under Shaka in Zululand.

1821: Mzilikazi rebels against Shaka Zulu by refusing to turn over cattle captured in a raid.

1821–1836: Mzilikazi flees, and he and his followers spread war and destruction across southern and western Africa. They raid towns, take cattle and captives, and strengthen the Ndebele military state, always defending their tribe from other tribes such as the Griquas, Hottentots, and Zulus.

1836: The Ndebele attack Boer trekkers, mistakenly thinking they are Griqua raiders. The Boers hit back hard using rifles, eventually sacking Mzilikazi's towns and confiscating many cattle. This last devastating rout sends the Ndebele north across the Limpopo, where they finally settle in Matabeleland, once the domain of the Changamire.

1868: Mzilikazi dies. Civil war erupts over the succession. Leadership eventually goes to Mzilikazi's son, Lobengula.

1880: The Ndebele population stands at 100,000, with an army of 20,000 disciplined spearmen.

1888: Lobengula signs the Rudd Concession which assigns to Cecil Rhodes exclusive mineral rights throughout the Ndebele kingdom in exchange for a £100 monthly stipend and 1,000 breech-loading rifles. Lobengula mistakenly understands that the rights limit foreign white penetration to ten miners under his royal authority. But soon a hand-picked group of 200 pioneers are granted 3,000 acres. A small mining reconnaissance thus becomes a major permanent colony.

1893: Ndebele raiders set fire to villages and take cattle in Mashona country. In October, Jameson, the South Africa Company's administrator, invades Matabeleland. Lobengula retreats northward toward the Zambezi, where he finally succumbs to a bout of smallpox. The war ends, and Matabeleland falls to the Company by right of conquest.

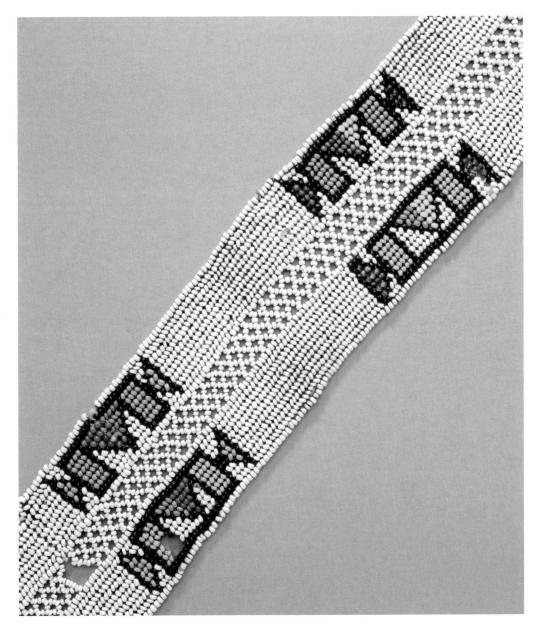

Antique blanket edging. Collection of Carol Perrenoud. 2¼" × 1' 1".

BEADING STYLE

Ndebele beaders work without patterns or instructions, keeping their techniques in their heads. This method says a lot about the time and energy they spend developing their skills. My United Kingdom Internet bead friend, Stephney Hornblow, was lucky enough to visit (and bead with!) the Ndebele. She and her fellow traveling beader, Evelyn Cohen, were generous enough to share some photos and beading techniques with me, so with their kind permission, I'd like to pass them along to you.

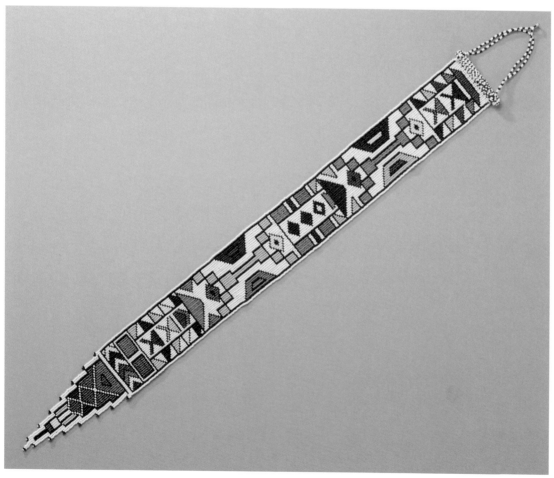

Contemporary wedding veil. Collection of Carol Perrenoud. 3½" × 2' 11½".

"LOVE LETTERS"

Girls make small beaded "love letters" to give to their suitors. Meaning is conveyed by the placement and use of color. Meanings vary from tribe to tribe, but here is one set of color messages:

Color	Positive meaning	Negative meaning
Black (Shadow)	Marriage, regeneration	Sorrow, despair, death
Blue (Dove)	Fidelity, request	Ill feeling, hostility
Yellow (Corn)	Wealth, industry	Withering away
Green (New grass)	Jealousy, lovesickness	Illness, discord
Pink (Poor one)	Oath	Poverty, laziness
Red (Blood)	Intense passion, love	Anger, heartache
Turquoise (Pigeon)	Loneliness, missing love	Impatience
Brown (Soil)	Nurturing or growing love	Emptiness, hunger
White (Bone)	Spiritual love, virginity, purity	

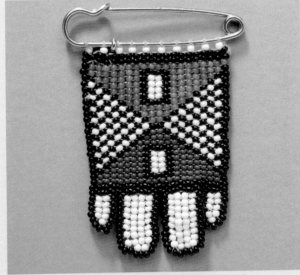

Love Letter. *Collection of Carol Perrenoud.*

Stephney and Evelyn visited with two different Ndebele groups, the Tshwaraganang beaders at Mimotla, and the women at the tourist village of Botshebelo. The people live and work here to show traditional Ndebele life and skills. The women of Botshebelo call herringbone stitch "sveni."

The Tshwaraganang beaders were given a small grant to start a bead business in an old dry cleaner's building. The co-op produces beadwork to sell to the tourist trade. During Stephney and Evelyn's visit, they were working on a large order for Christmas decorations

Stephney with beaders at Mimotla.

Wall decoration at Botshebelo.

Stephney at Botshebelo.

Wall decoration at Botshebelo.

Photos by Stephney Hornblow

made out of the balls from roll-on deodorants covered with lace-stitched beadwork. When Stephney brought out her beadwork to show, the ladies wanted her to teach them how to make her life-like lizard, because this is the form in which Ndebele ancestors return. Four days later, the beaders were selling their own beaded lizards at the Magnolia market!

The Beaders at Botshebelo bead instinctively, without rigid rules. If it works, it's okay! They sit with straight backs and outstretched

Photos by Stephney Hornblow

Stephney admiring Dina II's work in progress.

Dina I and Evelyn holding one of Dina's paintings.

legs, with a folded blanket on their laps to act as a beading tray. They pick up every dropped bead, because beads are precious. When Stephney asked Botshebelo beader Rita how a particular piece was made, Rita got out her scissors and started cutting it apart to figure it out. When she had it all figured out, the work was beautifully restored, and the stitches explained.

Both groups begin their beadwork with a foundation row of single needle ladder stitch

Beads in the Trees.

Photos by Stephney Hornblow

Ndebele hanging.

Contemporary bag from the museum in Botshelobo.

Photo by Stephney Hornblow

with a two-bead stack. (See the Techniques Section, pages 38–40 for further information.)

In Tshwaraganang, a beadworker named Elizabeth taught Stephney and Evelyn a row-end technique that uses a turn and a knot for each row.

Rita, at Botshebelo, taught a similar turn, but without the knot.

As you will see in the Techniques Section, each turn has its uses, especially when you're doing beadwork with uneven edges.

NDEBELE DESIGN

Ndebele homes are painted and decorated with stylized designs from the surrounding

Contemporary bag from the museum in Botshelobo.

Photo by Stephney Hornblow

world, such as safety razor blades, airplanes, and telephone poles. Originally, (and still, in the more remote areas) these paintings were done in ocher, dung, slaked lime, charcoal, and other organics, but bright acrylic paints are now used. Ndebele beadwork reflects these designs and colors, and it is used for traditional items such as aprons, headdresses, blanket edgings, and beadwork sold to tourists.

Using a safety razor blade as a design element started in the 1940s. The blades were

Tubular herringbone on necklace of tourist trade.

Detail.

Photo by Stephney Hornblow

first introduced to Africa where they were used to shave heads for funerals or special occasions. The women were given the dulled blades for trimming threads from their beadwork. The geometric shape provided inspiration for their wall decorations and beadwork, for which it now provides a characteristic look.

CLOTHING AND ACCESSORIES

Ndebele beaded garments signify specific traditions and the wearer's status within the tribe. Styles of aprons for women and girls include the lighabi, worn before marriage; the isiphetu, signifying availability for marriage; the liphotu, worn when first married and before children; and the ijogolo, the most important apron, which shows that the women have children and are thus valuable members of the tribe.

The Ndebele women wear a blanket when outdoors that is beaded along the edge according to the age and skill of the wearer. A woman will bead a piece for her blanket to commemorate significant events in her life and the life of her family. Beaded rings, called galwani, are circlets of grass wound with beads that are worn on the arms and legs as signs of wealth.

Ndebele women's wedding outfits consist of a goatskin or cloth cape (linga), a beaded veil, and a beaded stick, often shaped like a telephone pole. The liphotu apron has a main beaded panel with beaded tassels and ancillary panels on each side.

Women whose sons are initiated into the tribe wear "long tears" or linga koba. These panels signify the sorrow of losing a son to adulthood and the joy of his reaching manhood. They are worn suspended from a narrow headband and reach to the ground.

The fertility doll is made by mothers and daughters for young girls to keep during courtship and marriage. Once she has had her first baby, a young woman must destroy the doll because it is no longer needed. Nowadays, these dolls are frequently made for tourists.

SUPPLIES

Beading supplies don't change much from stitch to stitch, so I'll list enough for beginners to have all the basics, plus some goodies so experienced beaders won't be bored. This supply list constitutes what I use at this stage in my beading life.

Please check out the other beading books from Interweave Press for further discussion of bead characteristics, supplies, and tools.

BEADS AND DESIGN

The most important thing is, of course, the beads! I've done some simple patterns that turned out wonderfully because of the beads I used, and I've ruined some gorgeous patterns with the wrong beads. I've worked with seed beads as small as size 20° all the way up to size 3°, although I tend to use mostly size 11° seeds and Delicas. Color, finish, shape, and size all affect how the finished beadwork looks.

Use the best quality beads you can. Watch for beads that fade—your bead source can usually tell you if beads have been dyed or galvanized and whether the color will fade or rub off. You can set bead color with a clear spray such as Krylon®. Just put the beads in a plastic bag and spray in a few spritzes. Smoosh the beads around a couple of times as they are drying so they don't stick together. (Thanks to Suzanne Cooper for this tip.)

Magazine ads are a great place to find color schemes. Tear out that beautiful ad and match up your beads. If you have a hard time choosing colors, get a good book on color theory. (Try the library so you can save your cash for beads!) Look for books that include the effect of light as well as pigment colors, because beads are similar to stained glass in transmitting colors. The more you bead, the more you'll have an instinct for what works and what doesn't. You'll also find that you develop your own style. I sometimes challenge myself to use colors other than my favorites, but I have to be careful, because if I don't really love my colors, I never finish the project.

Evenly sized beads will result in evenly sized beadwork. Set the really fat and skinny beads aside for increases and decreases. Those beads that are way too crooked to use? Throw them over your shoulder for luck!

15° round

33 DB

8° Czech

11° Delica

11° 3-cut

9° 3-cut

11° Czech

I've beaded some samples with different sizes and shapes of beads to give you an idea how the various beads look when worked up in herringbone. Each beaded square is 10 by 10 beads.

When you're working a stitch, it's good to know how the beads will lie, and affect the pattern. Round beads seem to show less space in between and be more flexible than "square" beads like cylinder beads or twisted hex beads. (In contrast, square beads show less space in peyote stitch.) Herringbone stitch, like netting, is forgiving of slightly different bead sizes, so it's a great way to use those uneven 3-cuts!

The fact that beads sit in a specific angle in a herringbone pattern does affect the design. It's a little like bargello, or plastic canvas embroidery. Patterns for loomwork or square stitch, or even cross-stitch and other embroidery patterns, can be done in herringbone, but the proportions will be a little off, depending on the shape of the beads used. If in doubt, work up a sample before undertaking a large herringbone project adapted from another stitch.

There are great computer programs specifically designed for graphing beadwork patterns. Some even turn a photo into a pattern almost by magic! You can also use almost any general graphics program to draw the bead outlines and fill in different colors. Then there's always the old fashioned way—colored pencils and graph paper.

TOOLS

Basic beading tools include needle, thread, thread conditioner, scissors, beading surface, and light. Extras include a cigarette lighter, glue, a scoop of some type, flat-nosed pliers, needle grabber, and a box to keep everything in.

Needles

Needles should be chosen with thread AND bead sizes in mind. For herringbone, I like to use a regular beading needle in a size 10 or 12. Use the size that allows your thread to pass easily through the eye of the needle, as well as through the beads. Sharps are short needles that are great for getting into tight spaces, with the added benefit that they don't break as easily as the longer beading needles. A tapestry needle comes in handy for picking apart unwanted knots and tangles. (Don't you just hate it when that happens?)

Thread

The thread must pass comfortably through the beads at least four times to allow for tying off old threads and adding new. Also, take into account the use of the finished beadwork. Will it be worn and played with, like a

May be reproduced for personal use only.

necklace? Use strong heavy threads. Will the piece be primarily decorative? Use a lightweight, less sturdy thread. Does the piece need to be flexible? Use a thin thread so the beads have room to move. Does the piece need to be stiff? Fill the beads' holes with thread (use fat thread) and pull tight to help the beadwork be more rigid.

That said, thread is up to you! Experience will help you know your favorites. I use the Nymo® brand almost exclusively for my beadwork. I like its texture and ease of use, as well as its range of colors and weights. Most of the time I use a single strand of size B, and double it when I need more weight.

Thread Conditioner

Always coat your thread with some type of thread conditioner. It helps keep your thread from tangling, helps it to glide through the beads, and protects it from body oils and dirt. I like microcrystalline wax because it's stickier than regular beeswax. To wax your thread, thread your needle, hold the thread just below the eye of the needle with one hand, sandwich the thread between the

thumb of your other hand and the wax, and pull. I do this two or three times, then pull the thread between my fingers several times to warm the wax and help it soak into the thread, and also to remove any excess.

Scissors

Scissors can be any type of cutter that allows a sharp, smooth cut close to the beadwork. Embroidery scissors work well, and there are lots of other types of snips and cutters available.

Beading Surface

By beading surface, I mean the place where you pour out your beads to work from. If you pour them on a bare table, they'll just run away, and you'll spend a lot of time chasing them around! To make a beading surface on a tabletop, I used to use tea towels, huck toweling, and ultrasuede, but I've recently discovered Vellux®. This is the foamy, napped synthetic fabric that blankets and stuffed toys are made of. It's the best surface I've found so far. I use a neutral cream color, and I haven't yet used a bead that doesn't show up. The pile is deep enough to keep the beads from rolling around and escaping, but not so deep that the beads get lost. Your needle doesn't get caught in Vellux, as can happen with felt or tea towels. It's machine washable and dryable, in case you spill something on it, and it can be trimmed to fit your favorite tray or tool kit without fraying. Can you tell I really like it?

Lighting

As for light, I almost always bead by an Ott-Lite®. It's a brand of full-spectrum lightbulb that helps you to see the true colors of your beads, as in natural sunlight. It's bright, but doesn't generate too much heat. I use a folding tabletop Ott-Lite lamp. There is also a floor lamp model and lamps with a magnifier attached. There are other brands of full-spectrum lightbulbs out there to fit other existing lamps and light fixtures. I have one in my ceiling light in my bead room. It's amazing how much difference a good light makes in helping you to see those tiny beads and their even tinier holes, as well as in threading your needles.

Cigarette Lighter

A lighter comes in handy for melting that last little bit of thread that your scissors just couldn't reach. Trim your threads as close as possible, hold the lighted lighter (or match or candle) in one hand, and bring the beadwork close to the flame. You can watch the tiny tail shrink right away! Somewhere I read that you can also use a lighted stick of incense. When I tried that, though, it left a dirty ash smear on my beadwork, so I don't recommend this method. Matches take two hands to light, so you have to light the match, then pick up your beadwork, find the right spot, and melt the thread, all before the match goes out or burns your fingers! That's why I keep a small lighter in my beading tool kit.

Glue

I rarely glue a knot. I'm scared that I'll have to go through that area later and the bead holes will be filled with glue. When I feel I really need to glue a knot, I use GS Hypo-Tube® Cement or clear nail polish.

Bead Scoop

My favorite scoop is called a Scoopula®. It's a long curved tool, like a tube cut in half lengthwise, rounded on one end and pointy on the other. It's used in the medical profession. This little gadget is perfect for scraping up leftover beads and sliding them back in their tubes. I also have a little triangular aluminum tray that works well for scraping beads out of the carpet.

Flat-nosed Pliers

Another tool that comes in handy is a pair of flat-nosed pliers. Use them to grab a needle close to the beadwork and help to coax it through a tight spot. Try turning the needle as you pull, because some beads holes are oval-shaped and the needle will go through when turned just a little. Don't pull too hard, though, or something will give. It could be that the needle, the thread, or even the bead will break, and that's not good! You can also use your pliers to beak off a bead when you've added too many and don't want to do the frog stitch. (You all know what that is, right? When you have to "Rip it, Rip it, Rip it!") Just put the pliers across the hole of the bead and squeeze. When you do this, be sure to protect your eyes from flying glass bits. Also, there is always the risk of breaking the thread when you crush the bead, so be careful!

Needle Grabber

A wide rubber band, (like the kind that comes on broccoli) also works great to help you grab a needle, plus it doesn't take up so much room in your bead kit.

Beading Storage Box

I keep my favorite storage box handy. It's a small plastic divided box, filled with my supplies—lots of Nymo bobbins in different colors and sizes, needles, a lighter, a lump of microcrystalline wax, tiny scissors, a baby scoop, a sample-sized bottle of nail polish, and a rubber band. That way, I'm always ready to work on a project—all I need to do is pick out my beads, grab a Vellux pad, turn on the light, and bead! Someday, I should cover my tool kit with beads. . . .

TECHNIQUES

STRUCTURE OF HERRINGBONE STITCH

Herringbone beadwork appears to be worked ninety degrees from normal: that's the first thing you'll notice about this stitch. When I show beaders a piece of herringbone, you can see the gears turning in their beady brains as they try to figure out the stitch. When I turn it ninety degrees, and say "you work it THIS way," the light goes on!

The beads sit in regular columns of Vs or chevrons—hence the name herringbone. The beadwork is very flexible from side to side, allowing for narrow tubes, or folds for a purse, etc. But it is rather stiff top to bottom, especially if worked with square beads. Take advantage of this feature for the sides of vessels or boxes—they'll stand up nicely.

It's easy to switch from herringbone to double (two-drop) peyote stitch. Just add two beads between each column, instead of on top. Maybe this is how the stitch got started. Could an ancient beader have made a fortunate mistake while doing peyote stitch?

There are two methods for starting herringbone, one popularized by Virginia Blakelock in her book *Those Bad, Bad Beads* and one that I call the "ladder start." How you turn at the end of the row will depend on which start you use, whether you have an odd or even number of beads, and whether you are working up or down from the starting rows. I'll explain more thoroughly later on.

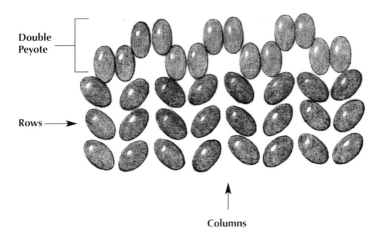

Double Peyote

Rows →

Columns

GETTING STARTED

You've picked out your beads, turned on the light, and have your pattern handy. Pull up a chair, snuggle onto the couch, or sit on the floor like the Ndebele. Pour little puddles of your chosen beads out onto your beading surface. No need to pour out the whole tube or hank. Just pour out about a spoonful for now. You can always add more.

Thread your needle. This is the hardest part of beadwork. Some tricks for easy threading include using sharp scissors to cut the thread at an angle, making sure you can see the eye of the needle, licking the eye of the needle as well as the thread, waxing the end of the thread, and "needling the thread" by pinching one end of the thread between your thumb and finger and putting the needle *on* the thread. Try all of the above methods, and if all else fails, have someone thread the needle for you!

Use the thread as it comes off the spool, and it will be better behaved and tangle less. Use a comfortable length for your project. This is usually about 4 feet for a single thread or 3 yards if you're going to double it. I thread the needle, unroll the required amount, and then cut the thread.

Next, condition your thread. (See page 30 for directions.)

Now add a tension or stopper bead by stringing one bead, pulling it to about 6 inch- es from the tail end of your thread, and tying a single overhand knot. Alternatively, you can pass through the bead again in the same di- rection. This stopper bead keeps the rest of your beads from escaping as you work, yet it can easily be removed when you no longer need it. It is not counted as part of your pat- tern or beadwork. Unless otherwise stated, always start your beadwork in this manner. The following directions and projects all as- sume a stopper bead.

FLAT HERRINGBONE STITCH

I learned this first start method from Virginia Blakelock's book, *Those Bad, Bad Beads*. She states that she and her partner, Carol Perre- noud, figured it out from finished South African beadwork with a magnifying glass and experimentation. I call it the triple-row start because you work the first three rows right off. It's my favorite because it gives the most even spacing. The tension is a little tricky at first, but your patience will pay off. When just learning, use three different colors for this start so you can see the mechanics of the stitch.

Rows 1 and 2: String 1 lavender, *2 purple, 2 lavender. Repeat from the * until all the first and second row beads have been strung, then finish by stringing a lavender bead. You'll have multiples of 4 beads.

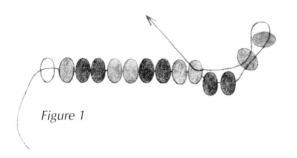

Figure 1

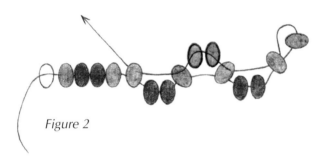

Figure 2

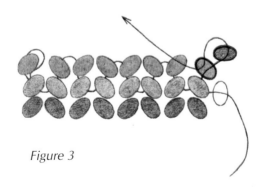

Figure 3

Row 3: String 1 teal to add the first bead of the third row. Turn and pass back through the last lavender bead you strung for Rows 1 and 2. Skip 2 (first row) beads and pass through the next (second row) bead on your thread, heading toward the tail (Figure 1).

This start method needs a little slack, so, depending on the width of your beadwork, leave room at the end of the thread between the working beads and the stopper bead. Half the length of the beads you've strung (one row's length) seems to be about right. You can always slide the stopper bead down a little if you need more room, but be sure you have enough of a tail to tie off.

*Add 2 teal beads, pass through the next bead (towards the tail), skip 2 beads, and pass through the next bead (towards the tail). Pull on both the needle and the tail threads *evenly* to tighten. This is the secret to getting the first rows to lie right (Figure 2). Repeat from * to the end of the row.

You should now have a twisty string of Vs. If you keep the string of Vs lined up as you work, the next row is much easier. Use your thumbnail to help the beads sit on top of each other and spread out in a V shape.

Row 4: Add the last Row 3 bead (teal) and the first Row 4 bead (purple). Turn and pass back through the last 2 beads of Row 3 (Figure 3).

You'll notice that, with this turn, the thread shows at every other bead on the side edges. It doesn't usually bother me, but you can always add camouflage by coloring any thread that's obvious with a permanent marker in the appropriate color.

Add 2 purple beads and pass through the next 2 beads from Row 3. Point your needle down through the first bead and up through the second. Keep beading across the row in this manner. The beadwork is starting to take shape! (Figure 4.)

Remember that turns are done by adding the last bead of the current row and the first bead of the next row, and passing back through the last bead of the current row and the next-to-last bead of the current row. To bead, add 2 beads, pass through 2 beads.

When you have a few rows done you can tighten the first row, if necessary. Working from the edge opposite the tail, pull on the beadwork 2 beads at a time, all across the bottom of the piece (Figure 5).

To finish your beadwork, just add the one last bead, and tie off your thread.

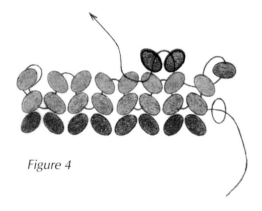

Figure 4

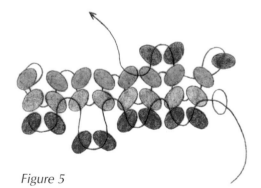

Figure 5

LADDER STITCH START

You can also start your herringbone with a row of ladder stitch, the same way you start brick-stitched beadwork. Since herringbone is beaded in pairs, make your ladder an even number of beads long.

There are two ways to create a ladder. With the first method, called back stitch, the thread crisscrosses through the beads, going through each bead twice. It leaves less thread in the beads but it's more rigid than the next method.

The second way, called a single-needle ladder, makes it easier for the herringbone-stitched beads to move into their chevrons. The thread spirals through the beads and passes through each bead three times. Make sure your beads have big enough holes if you're going to make your ladder this way.

Since the tension and bead spacing are tighter in the ladder than in the triple row herringbone start—regardless of which technique you use, some beaders create a ladder as a temporary foundation, and then cut it off later. Or you can use a ladder start to give a vessel or box edge a little extra stiffness.

Back-Stitched Ladder Start Method

Row 1: String all the beads for your first row. Leave a space equal to about half the length of your beads. Pass through the second bead from your needle, going in the same direction as the beads were strung. When you pull up on both threads, the two beads will sit nicely next to each other with their holes parallel (Figure 1).

Pass through the next bead, again in the same direction, and pull it up to sit next to the other two (Figure 2).

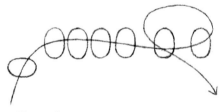

Figure 1

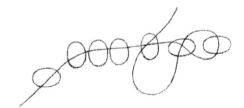

Figure 2

Repeat until all your beads are used up and you have a ladder of beads sitting side by side (Figure 3).

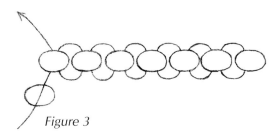

Figure 3

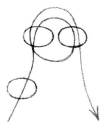

Figure 1

Keep your thread tension a little loose to allow the beads to tilt into their columns of Vs on the next row. The trick here is to be absolutely sure you don't split any threads. You can slide your stopper bead up next to the beadwork to help hold the tension while you work on the next rows.

Figure 2

Single-Needle Ladder Start Method

Row 1: This method allows the beads to tilt more easily, but it puts an additional thread through the holes.

String 2 beads. Make a circle by passing through the first and second beads, again in the same direction (Figure 1).

String 1 bead. Go down through the second and up through the third bead (Figure 2).

Continue adding single beads and sewing through them in a circular path until you reach the desired length.

You can also make any style of ladder with a 2 or 3 or more bead tall stack.

If you are using all the same color beads for your first 2 rows, you can just flip the beadwork around until the thread is coming out the top, and continue. If you're following a pattern, you'll end up with your thread com-

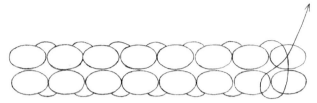

Figure 3

ing out the bottom of the strip of beads. Go up the second to last bead on the bottom row, then up through the last bead on the top row to get your thread into position to continue (Figure 3).

Rows 2 and up: Regardless of how you did the first row, the next row is the same. String the first pair of beads of the second row. Go down through the second bead on the base row, and up through the third bead on the base row (Figure 4).

*String the next pair of beads of the second row. Go down through the next bead on the base row, and up through the following bead on the base row. Repeat from * across.

TURNS

Ladder Turn

When you start with a ladder, you'll notice that you don't have an extra bead on each end to turn with. To turn, simply catch the loop of thread from the first row, and go back up the same bead, just like brick stitch. This is also the way to turn when you're working down (instead of up) from the triple-row start.

Figure 4

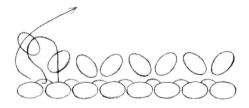

Ladder turn

Rita's Turn

When you pull up the thread, this turn gives the same result as catching the top thread. Go down through the last bead of the previous row, and wrap your working thread around the core thread below it, then go back up the last 2 edge beads.

Elizabeth's Turn

With its knot, this turn adds a security feature, because if your thread breaks at a later date, only one row can unravel. Simply go down through the last bead of the previous row and tie a knot with your working thread around the core thread below it, (see Adding New Thread on page 44) then go back up the last 2 edge beads.

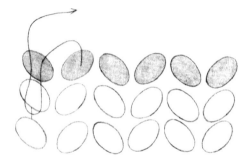

Rita's turn

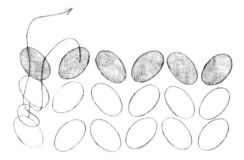

Elizabeth's turn

TUBULAR HERRINGBONE

When you're working tubular herringbone stitch with the triple row start, the trickiest part is leaving enough slack to allow your beads to tilt, but not so much that thread is left over when you've gone all the way around. It's easiest to use this method for small tubes and save the ladder start for large tubes. For large tubes I've recently been doing the first 4 rows flat, and then joining them into a tube, because it's easier when starting a tube that's bigger that 8 or 10 beads around. Just sew down, then up the edge beads, zigzagging from one side to the other.

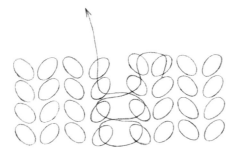

Joining flat herringbone

Triple-Row Start Tube

String a multiple of 4 beads. Connect them into a circle by going through the first 2 beads. *Add 2 beads, sew through the next bead on the ring, skip 2 beads, sew through the next bead on the ring. Repeat from the *, all the way around.

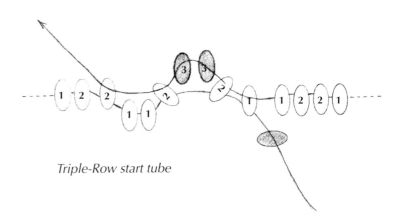

Triple-Row start tube

The Step Up

This tube will always have a "step up" at the end of a row. To make the step up, go up through the first bead of the second (or previous) round and the first bead of the third (or current) round. Remember, that first circle of beads is really the first two rounds! Now you're ready for the next round.

If you've been very careful not to split any threads, you can tighten things up at this point.

The Step Up

Ladder Tube

Create a ladder using your favorite method, as in the previous section. Join the two ends of the ladder to make a ring by sewing through the end beads several times, knotting if necessary. Check to make sure that the ladder is not twisted before you tie any knots.

Bead around the ring, as with flat herringbone. When you get to the end of the round, there will be a step up. Add your last 2 beads, go down though the base row bead, and up through 2 beads (the first previous round bead, and the first bead of this round). Watch for this step up on each round, because if you lose it, you'll have a hard time creating a pattern or ending the beadwork evenly. If you're doing freeform sculptural herringbone, you won't need to worry about the step up. It will disappear as if by magic.

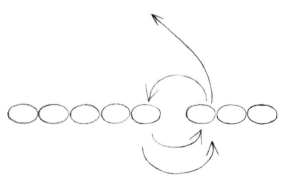

Joining ladder ends

Tubular Variations

You can play with thread paths to create different looks. If you go down through one bead and up through two each time, your tube will lean and begin to spiral.

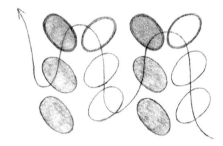

Creating a spiral

You can go down through 2 and up through 1 to spiral in the other direction.

TYING OFF AND ADDING NEW THREAD

Most beaded items require more than one needleful of thread. So, when your thread gets down to about 4 inches, it's time to tie off the old and add a new thread. The first time you add new thread, you can also tie off the tail (after you've tied off your working thread and before you add new thread). Remember to remove the stopper bead if you used one.

It's easiest to tie off and add new thread in the middle of a row. Do it like so: *go down through a few beads. Tie an overhand knot around the core thread by bringing your needle from the front to the back and then from the back to the front (catching the core thread just below the bead your working thread is coming out of).

Leave a small loop of thread on the front side (Figure 1).

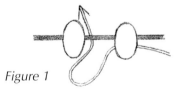

Figure 1

Figure 2

Put your needle through the loop from right to left, and pull everything up tight (Figure 2).

Follow the thread path, and repeat from the * at least twice more. I like to change direction a couple of times for added security (Figure 3). Cut the thread off as close to the work as possible.

Start your new thread 2 columns back and 4 or 5 beads down from where you tied off, and tie on in the same way (Figure 4). See why it's easier to tie off in the middle of the row? That way you don't run into any knots from tying off and on in the same area.

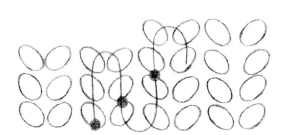

Figure 3

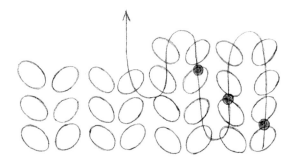

Figure 4

Figure 1

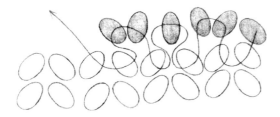

Figure 2

Figure 3

INCREASING

There are lots of ways to increase your herringbone beadwork. You can increase within the beadwork, creating ruffles or bumps in the body of the work. You can force a rapid increase, or work a gradual increase over several rows. You can increase within the columns (I'll abbreviate this as W inc), or between the columns (B inc). You can also increase on the edges to change the outline of the work.

Between the Columns Increase (*B inc*)

To increase rapidly within herringbone you can force 2 beads between the 2-bead columns on one row, and then incorporate the 2 beads into your herringbone on the next (Figure 1).

Increase every other column for a very ruffled edge.

For a gradual increase, add 1 bead between the columns on 1 row (Figure 2), then add 2 beads at that place on the next (Figure 3); on the third row of the increase, incorporate the 2 beads into your herringbone.

If you increase 1 bead between each column, 2 beads on the next row, then 3 beads, and so on, it creates a dragon-wing effect (Figure 4). Don't incorporate the increases into the herringbone, leave them as free-floating strands.

Figure 4

Work this increase from a 5 or 6 column tube, and you get a morning glory type flower (Figure 5).

Figure 5

Within the Column Increase (*W inc*)

Add 3 beads instead of 2 (Figure 6), then add 2 beads between each of the 3 on the

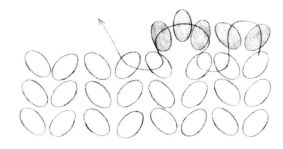

Figure 6

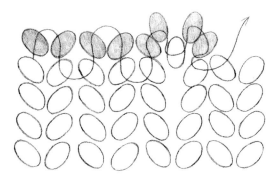

Figure 7

next row (Figure 7), finally incorporating them into your stitching (Figure 8).

Edge Increase

To increase on the outside edges, ladder stitch beads onto the end of the desired row, (use the single-needle method on page 39) then turn and bead back across. If you add multiples of 2 beads, the turns will remain the same, but if you add an odd number of beads, the turns will change to the alternate method (from a triple row turn to a brick stitch turn, or vice versa) (Figure 9).

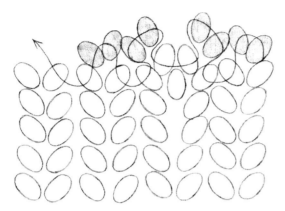

Figure 8

Figure 9

If you want to increase on both edges on the same row, just ladder stitch to one edge, then bead back across. When you get to the opposite edge, make a ladder that's 2 beads high, with the second bead lining up *under* the first (Figure 10). That way the increase will start at the same row on each side.

Turn, do another W inc, and bead across the row and back (Figure 12).

Figure 12

Figure 10

Herringbone Curl

If you make a W inc in the last column on one edge on every row, your beadwork will form a shell-like curl (Figure 11).

Repeat this turn on every row, and your beadwork will make a sharp curl. For a more gradual curl, increase on every other row (i.e., W inc, turn, and bead back across the row). See Figure 13.

Figure 11

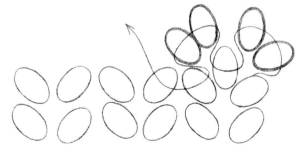

Figure 13

Herringbone Curl by Vicki Star.

DECREASING

To decrease, work the previous methods in reverse. It's like taking a dart in fabric, causing the beadwork to narrow.

Between the Column Decrease

To decrease rapidly within the beadwork you can run your thread through a 2-bead column without adding any beads on one row, and then completely skip them on the next (Figure 1). Pull your thread really tight to close up any spaces and prevent thread from showing.

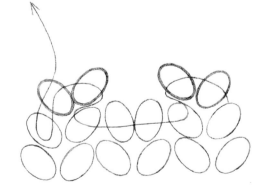

Figure 1

For a gradual decrease, add only 1 bead (instead of 2) on one row (Figure 2). On the next row of the decrease, skip that bead completely.

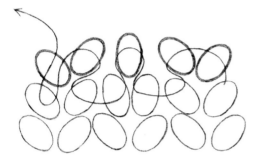

Figure 2

On the next row, add only 2 beads on top of the 3 you added (Figure 4).

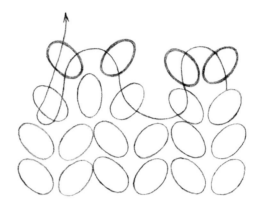

Figure 4

Here, 3 columns have turned into 2. Be sure to pull your thread tight!

Within the Column Decrease

Go up the first bead of 1 column, add 3 beads, and go down through the second bead of the second column on the first row of this decrease (Figure 3).

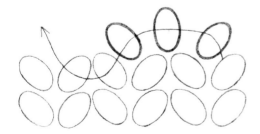

Figure 3

Edge Decrease

To decrease on the edge, simply turn around early, using the turning method necessary (Figure 5).

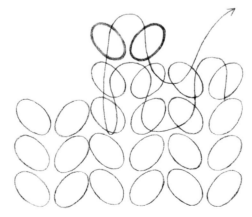

Figure 5

CIRCULAR HERRINGBONE

Start with a ring of beads (Figure 1), then add 1 bead between each (Figure 2), and then 2 beads between each of those (Figure 3).

Increase using the gradual or rapid methods, depending on how flat or curved you want your piece (Figure 4).

Figure 1

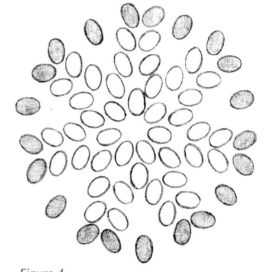

Figure 4

Figure 2

Figure 3

To keep the circle even, increase in regular increments around the ring. As with tubular herringbone, you must watch for the step up. You can use a bit of different colored thread for a row marker, as knitters do.

If you stop increasing, but keep beading, the beadwork will eventually turn into a straight-sided tube. This takes several rows to become apparent. Pull the thread tight on each row until the beads behave!

ARC HERRINGBONE

By using graduated sizes of beads, you can create a C-shaped piece of beadwork. I first saw this method used for fabulous beaded collars done by Carole Horn. The height of the beads makes this technique work. Stack the same number of each bead (say 10 or 12) on a needle to see how they relate. Stick each needle into a pincushion, and line up the towers of beads according to height.

Make a single needle ladder for the first row. Use one or two of each size bead, in order, from shortest to tallest. Now bead back across the row from tallest to shortest. Always use the same size above each bead. You'll see the beadwork magically curve as you bead. Create a fan shape and sew it into a cone to make a bowl or vessel, or keep going to make a nearly complete circle for a collar.

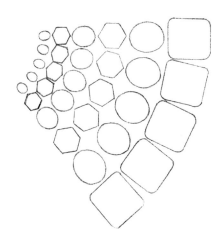

Beaded Fan Book by Vicki Star.

FINISHING HERRINGBONE

A nice way to finish the top and bottom edges of herringbone stitch is to add a bead between every other bead all the way across. This "picot" edge straightens the herringbone edges, makes them lie flat, and helps to even out the tension on a wobbly first row. It also provides a great foundation row for netting or other stitches.

You can finish the last row with 3 beads at a time to automatically create the picot in one step instead of two.

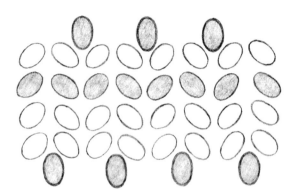

Using 14's w/ Delicas or 11's won't make picots, but it will make a neat Line.

PROJECTS

CARD CASE

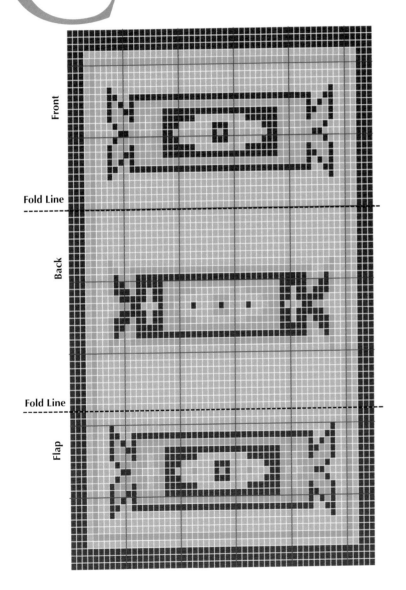

Front

Fold Line

Back

Fold Line

Flap

This little card case is my ode to the Ndebele. I created the design to be reminiscent of their designs, but I used VERY non-traditional colors. It's just big enough for business cards or a credit card and your driver's license.

MATERIALS

Size 11° Japanese seed beads in 3 colors (wine red with a blue luster, dusty pink lined crystal, muted green lined)
2 accent beads (6 to 8 mm) with large holes
Beading thread (I used size B Nymo—if you use different thread, you may have to use it single instead of double.)

Notions
Size 12 beading needles
Scissors
Thread conditioner

Step 1: Your card case will get a lot of wear, so use a doubled thread. Start with about 4 yards of thread (that's 2 yards after doubling) because the first few rows take up a lot of thread. Remember to condition your thread.

Step 2: Tie a stopper bead on the end of your thread, leaving a 6" tail. String 150 red

beads. Leave about 6" between the working beads and the stopper bead. This group of beads on your thread will become the first two rows of the beadwork.

Step 3: String 1 red bead. (This bead is the first bead of the third row.) Skip the bead just added and sew through the next bead, toward the tail. Skip 2 beads and pass through the next bead.

It's very important that you not split any threads. If you do, the beads can't pull up correctly.

Step 4: String 2 red beads and pass through the next bead. Skip 2 beads, pass through the third bead.

Step 5: *String 2 beads and pass through the next bead. Skip 2 beads and pass through the next one. Repeat from the * all the way across. You can use your thumbnail to help the beads "fold" into place.

Try to keep the beads fairly straight, but don't worry too much about how they lay; the next row pulls them into place. It's important to keep the tension the same on both the tail and needle threads. If you pull too much on either one, the beads won't lay right.

When you get to the end of the row, string 2 red beads—the last bead of row 3, and the first bead of row 4. (You are adding the last bead of the current row and the first bead of the next row.)

Skip the first red bead, and pass through the next red bead (the one that you just strung). Bring your needle through the first bead of the next two-bead set. To snuggle the beads up tight, hold the last bead between your thumb and finger, and pull on the thread.

Flip your beadwork over and work across the row, adding 2 beads and going down through 1 bead, then up through the next bead (those added on the previous row) all the way across. Be sure to follow the pattern, alternating between left to right, and right to left.

Turn and keep on beading, always adding 2 beads and going through 2 beads. (You'll add only 1 bead for the very last bead of the case.)

Once you've beaded the case "fabric," add a 1-bead picot edging (page 55) along the flap and back edges (see Pattern).

Step 6: Now fold up the front of your card case on the fold line. Join the edges by connecting the front edge to the single bead from the back edge. One side will have a single bead at the bottom corner (Figure 1).

Step 7: Add a 4-bead tubular spiral handle to the top left corner. Start with a 4-bead-long, 2-bead stacked ladder alternating 2 red and 2 pink beads. Join the ends of the ladder into a tube.

Bead around the tube, going up through 1 bead, and down through 2, always adding a light bead above light beads, and a dark bead above dark beads (Figure 2).

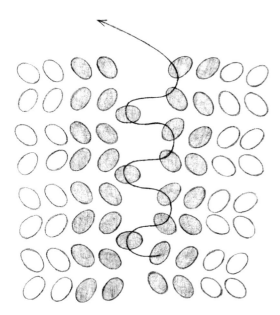

Figure 1

Figure 2

Don't worry about the step up, just keep spiraling around. Make your handle about 8" long—long enough to fit over your hand. You'll have to add new thread, but don't tie off the tail thread just yet. When the handle is long enough, thread a needle onto the starting tail and use it to connect the ends, then tie it off. Leave the needle thread attached so you can sew your handle to the purse.

To join the ends of the tube, fold the ends flat against each other (as opposed to joining the ends in a smooth tube as you would for a bangle bracelet) and stitch back and forth through beads. It doesn't matter how you accomplish this, just so the thread shows as little as possible.

Using the needle thread, pass through your accent bead and into a bead on the upper corner of the case. Sew back and forth, through the ends of the tube and the corner of the case until you can't fit through the beads. Tie off your thread.

TASSEL

I used a special Tassel Tool by Judy Walker (see Sources) to make a looped tassel for this project.

Set up your starting threads. Start with about 18" of thread and double it. Tape each end to the top crossbar of the tassel tool. Thread your needle and tape the thread to the crossbar, leaving about a 6" tail. String the following beads: 3 red, 21 pink, 1 green, 3 pink, 21 red, 3 pink, 1 green, 21 pink, 3 red. Tie a half-hitch knot around the crossbar and threads and string the next loop the same way. Each time you finish one loop, tie another half-hitch around the bar. Make 9 loops.

Carefully take off the tape, slide the tassel from the tool, and find the doubled thread that you started with. Put the loose ends through the looped end, and pull everything up tight. Now divide all but the needle threads in two and tie a couple of square knots. Trim and singe the ends, being extra careful not to harm the threads with the needle attached. If fire scares you, you can put a drop or two of glue on the knot, after you've attached the tassel to the case.

Sew through the other accent bead, pulling up the knot to hide inside, and attach it to the opposite corner (from the handle) of the card case. Again, sew back and forth until you can't fit any more threads, and tie off.

If you want your case to be more secure, you can sew a small piece of Velcro® under the flap to keep it closed. You can loop your case through a belt loop, or carry it around your wrist.

Tenth Kingdom Kaleidoscope

This magical kaleidoscope got its name because I did a lot of the beading while watching *The Tenth Kingdom* on television. They showed the whole miniseries in a ten-hour marathon! For those of you who've not seen it, it's a modern-day compilation of classical fairy tales. I just loved the Wolf!

I used a plain tubular cardboard kaleidoscope with a clear marble in the end. Since my kaleidoscope was red, I covered the tube with gold hologram paper. The paper shows a little between the AB finished gold beads, and it adds a subtle shimmer.

Do a little experimenting to figure out how many beads fit around your kaleidoscope, and make sure it's an even number. I did several trial strips before I started the actual project.

Materials

1" × 10" plain tube kaleidoscope
Size 11° gold-lined crystal AB, matte gold AB
Size B white beading thread
Hologram paper and double-sided tape or glue (optional)

Notions
Size 12 sharps needles
Thread conditioner
Scissors

Step 1: With matte gold beads, work a strip of flat herringbone 4 rows tall; the strip should fit around the kaleidoscope. When you finish the first 4 rows, join the edges to make a tube (Figure 1).

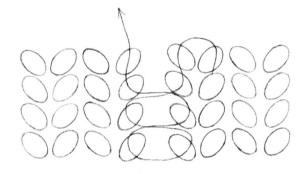

Figure 1

Step 2: Slide your herringbone tube onto the kaleidoscope, and continue working the tube in herringbone stitch, creating a random spiral pattern of shiny and matte gold beads. For example, in the fifth

round, I added shiny gold beads in a random pattern of 3 shiny, 2 matte, 5 shiny, 3 matte, etc. On the subsequent rounds, follow your pattern by adding whatever bead sits just below and to the right. Work off the end of the kaleidoscope, and keep sliding the beadwork tube up as you go (Figure 2). Watch for the step ups!

Figure 2

Step 3: Use all matte beads for the last 4 rounds. Bead to just over the edge of the marble and end with a picot edge. Go back to the bottom edge and add a new thread. Decrease on the bottom edge to help the beadwork curl a little over the end of the kaleidoscope (enough to cover the cardboard tube). Add a picot edge to finish it.

VIOLETS

Violets are my birth-flower—I was born in February—and I've always loved them. For this project I made about fifteen in different shades of purple, but I didn't use them all. I wonder where I can sew the rest of them?

MATERIALS

Size 11˚ seed beads in 3 different purples and 1 green

Size 8˚ opaque yellow seed beads

Size B white, purple, and green beading thread

Notions

Size 12 sharps needles

Thread conditioner

Scissors

Step 1: You need only about 18" of thread for each flower. Use a single thread and start with a single-bead tall ladder 12 beads long. I used the back-stitched ladder because the thread has to go through these beads lots of times.

Step 2: Work 6 herringbone stitches (Figure 1). Working on the opposite side of the ladder, add 6 single bead picots (Figure 2).

Step 3: Work 2 herringbone stitches, *pass through to the ladder and pass back up, then add 2 beads. Repeat from * 4 times. Turn. Note the beginnings of one wide petal, and four narrow ones (Figure 3).

Step 4: Work a 3-bead picot, pass all the way through to the ladder and back up. Repeat 4 times. Work 2 herringbone stitches and pass all the way down through the ladder (Figure 4).

Figure 1

Figure 2

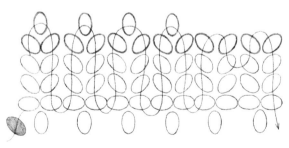

Figure 3

Figure 4

Step 5: Remove the stopper bead. Join the ladder to make a tube, then pass up through the edge of the wide petal and add a 1 bead B inc. Pass down through the other edge of the wide petal. Gather the flower by sewing through the single beads on the bottom of the ladder, tying knots as needed to maintain tension (Figure 5).

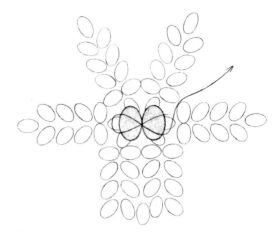

Figure 6

Figure 5

Step 6: Bring your thread out the center front of the flower, string 2 or 3 yellow beads, pass down though a bead on the other side of the center, and tie a knot or two to hold. Pass back through the center beads again to reinforce. Tie off the tail thread, but leave other thread attached to sew the flower to the kaleidoscope (Figure 6).

LEAVES

Make 4 or 5 of these little leaves.

Step 1: You need only about 18" of thread for each leaf. Using a single thread, start with a single-bead tall ladder 8 beads long. Use the back-stitch method.

Step 2: Work 1 herringbone on top, 1 on bottom, 2 on top, 1 on bottom, 1 on top. Turn. (See Figure 1.)

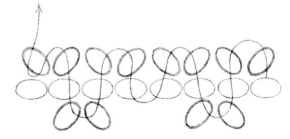

Figure 1

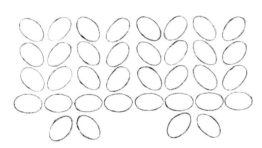
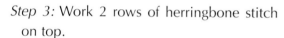

Figure 2

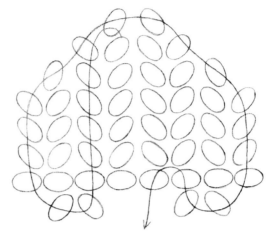

Figure 3

Step 3: Work 2 rows of herringbone stitch on top.

Step 4: Work 3 rows with a 1-bead decrease on each edge (Figure 2).

Step 5: Run your thread around and through the edge to align the beads. Pull tight to cause the leaf to cup. Come out the center bottom and tie off the tail thread, but leave the other thread attached to sew the leaf to the kaleidoscope (Figure 3).

ASSEMBLING THE KALEIDOSCOPE

When you've made all your flowers and leaves, arrange them on the table in pretty clusters, then transfer them to the scope, one at a time. Use the threads left on each one to sew through beads, back and forth from the kaleidoscope to the flower or leaf, until they're anchored securely.

This part takes patience, since there are lots of petals that want to catch and tangle your thread. You also want to be sure that your thread is hidden. Just take your time and watch your thread closely as you pull it up! It's lots easier with a short needle at this stage, because long ones tend to break as you try to force them through those awkward angles. Flat-nosed pliers come in handy to grab the needle and to help coax it through tight spots.

These nesting vessels help you learn how to increase for circular herringbone. Start with circular herringbone, change to even tubular herringbone, and then add increases on the top edge. Use the same concept to make larger vessels.

You must step up on each round. If you find you're having trouble figuring out which round you're on, and when to step up, count out the beads for each round ahead of time. That way, when you're out of beads, it's time for the next round. If you're still getting lost, try beading each round with a different color until you master the technique.

MATERIALS

7-Bead Vessel
Size 11° seed beads in 1 color
7 drops for accents
Size B beading thread

9-Bead Vessel
Size 11° seed beads in 2 colors
3 or 9 optional accent beads
Size B beading thread

Top
1 large bead big enough to sit on top of the 7-bead vessel without falling in, with a large enough hole to accept 18-gauge wire
18-gauge wire
Other accent beads, as desired

Notions
Size 12 needles
Thread conditioner
Scissors
Wire cutters
Flat-nosed pliers
Round-nosed pliers

7-BEAD CHEVRON VESSEL

Round 1: String 7 beads, pass through all of them again, and then pass through 1 more bead to make a ring.

Round 2: Add 1 bead between each bead all the way around, for a total of 7 beads.

Round 3: Add 2 beads between each bead for a total of 14 beads.

Round 4: Add 2 beads between each set of 2 to make a herringbone addition of 14 beads (Figure 1).

Round 5: Add 2 beads to each bead for a total of 28 beads (Figure 2).

Round 6: Add 2 beads between each set of 2 to make a herringbone addition of 28 beads (Figure 3).

Rounds 7–25: Repeat Round 6 to create 18 more rounds. Pull your thread tight to make the beads pull up into a tube. It takes several rows for the tube to become apparent, so don't give up! Remember to step up on each round.

Once your little vessel is tall enough (you could make a really tall vessel by working more rounds) add the embellishments around the top edge.

Figure 1

Figure 2

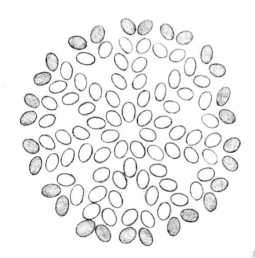

Figure 3

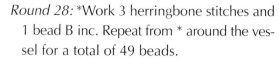

Round 26: *Add 2, pass through 1, add 1, and pass through 1. Repeat from * around the vessel for a total of 42 beads. This makes a 1-bead B inc between each column.

Round 27: *Work 1 herringbone stitch, a 2-bead B inc, 1 herringbone stitch, and a 1-bead B inc (Figure 4). Repeat from * around the vessel for a total of 49 beads.

Round 28: *Work 3 herringbone stitches and 1 bead B inc. Repeat from * around the vessel for a total of 49 beads.

Round 29: *Work 3 herringbone stitches and pass through 1 (the 1-bead B inc added on the last round) (Figure 5). Repeat from * around the vessel for a total of 42 beads.

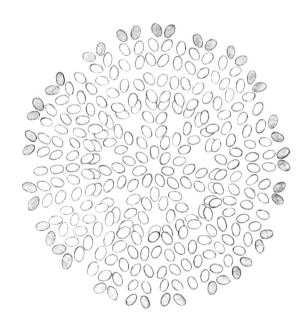

Figure 5

Figure 4

Round 30: *Add a 1-bead picot (to the first herringbone stitch of Round 22) and pass through 2. Add 2 beads, 1 drop, and 2 beads. Pass through 2 and add a 1-bead picot. Go down through 2, through 1, up through 2. Repeat from * around the vessel for a total of 42 beads, 7 drops (Figure 6).

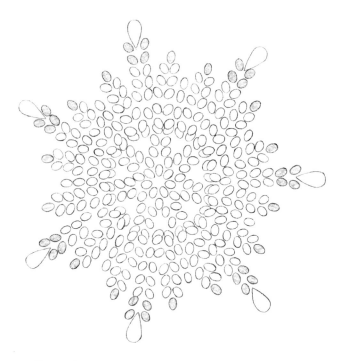

Figure 6

9-Bead Chevron Vessel

This outer vessel is made the same way as the 7-Bead Vessel, but the bead count is different. Also, it's made with two colors to give it vertical stripes. Remember your step ups!

Round 1: Make a ring of 3 beads.

Round 2: Add 1 bead between each for a total of 3 beads.

Round 3: Add 2 beads between each for a total of 6 beads.

Round 4: *Add 1 bead, pass through 1 bead, add 2 beads, pass through 1 bead (Figure 1). Repeat from * 2 times for a total of 9 beads.

Figure 1

Round 5: Add 1 bead between each for a total of 9 beads (Figure 2).

Round 6: Add 2 beads between each for a total of 18 beads.

Round 7: Work herringbone stitch all the way around for a total of 18 beads (Figure 3).

Round 8: *Work 1 herringbone stitch, then a 1-bead B inc of the contrasting color. Repeat from * 8 times for a total of 27 beads.

Round 9: *Work 1 herringbone stitch, then a 2-bead B inc of the contrasting color. Repeat from * 8 times for a total of 36 beads (Figure 4).

Figure 2

Figure 3

Figure 4

Round 10: Work herringbone stitch all the way around, following the color sequence established in Rounds 8 and 9. This round will have a total of 36 beads.

Rounds 11 through 25: * Repeat Round 10 for 14 rounds or to reach your desired height. Remember to pull your thread tight to encourage the beads to sit up and form a tube.

Add the embellishments around the top edge:

Round 26: *Add 1 main color bead picot, then work 5 herringbone stitches. Repeat from * 2 times, following the color sequence, for a total of 33 beads (Figure 5).

Round 27: *Pass through 3 beads, then work 5 herringbone stitches. Repeat from * 2 times, following the color sequence, for a total of 30 beads.

Round 28: * Pass through 5 beads, add a 1-bead picot, work 3 herringbone stitches, and add a 1-bead picot. Repeat from * 2 times, following the color sequence, for a total of 24 beads (Figure 6).

Round 29: *Pass through 7 beads (If the holes in the beads you've been going through are too full, work your thread down and around through other beads to hide it. As long as your thread comes out ready to work the next "petal" you'll be fine!), add a 1-bead

Figure 5

Figure 6

picot, add a 3-bead picot, and add a 1-bead picot. Repeat from * 2 times, following the color sequence, for a total of 15 beads.

Add drops or other embellishment on this round as desired.

TOP

To make a top for your chevron vessels, start with about 8" of 18-gauge wire. Make a spiral on one end, then string on your large accent bead or beads. Bend the wire coming out the top into a fancy shape and trim off any extra wire.

BELL EARRINGS

Follow the vessel pattern using size 14° seed beads with a 5-bead ring to start and you'll end up with sweet little bell earrings. You can add fringe (See the Fuchsia Earrings on page 78) or sew a larger bead in the center of the bell. A series of tiny vessels makes a wonderful lily-of-the-valley when done in white beads.

FUCHSIA EARRINGS

Remember those darling dancing flowers in the Disney movie, *Fantasia*? These lifelike flowers use lots of different increases and decreases. Make a pair for earrings, or create a cluster to hang from a tassel or a lariat necklace.

You'll work this flower from the top of the pink part all the way down to the purple inner petals. Then you'll come back to the middle and work the outer pink petals separately. Next, you'll come back up to the top to add the green calyx and hanging loop. And finally, you'll add the stamens.

MATERIALS

Size 11° bright pink Czech seed beads
Size 11° purple Japanese seed beads
Size 9° green three-cut seed beads
Size 12° yellow three-cut seed beads
Size 2 pink twisted bugles
Size B white beading thread
Ear wires

Notions
Size 12 beading needles
Thread conditioner
Scissors
Pliers

TOP OF FLOWER

Use all pink beads.

Step 1: Create a ring by stringing 8 beads. Pass through them again to make a circle, then pass through 1 more bead.

Step 2: Work 4 rounds of herringbone stitch (Figure 1). Pull your thread tight to help the

Figure 1

beads form a tube (Figure 2). Since this is an even tube, you must step up through 2 beads on each round.

Figure 2

Step 3: Work 1 round of herringbone stitch with a 1-bead B inc between every column for a total of 12 beads. Step up. This step makes a little bulge in the top of the flower (Figure 3).

Figure 3

Step 4: Work 1 round of herringbone stitch with a 1-bead B dec between every column for a total of 8 beads (Figure 4). Step up.

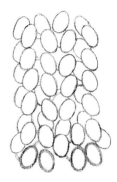

Figure 4

Step 5: Work 1 more round of herringbone stitch for a total of 8 beads (Figure 5). Step up.

Figure 5

INNER PETALS

Use all purple beads.
Step 6: Work 1 round of herringbone stitch (Figure 6). Step up.

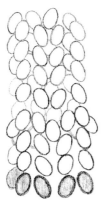

Figure 6

Step 7: Work 1 round of herringbone stitch with a 1-bead B inc between every column for a total of 12 beads (Figure 7). Step up.

Figure 7

Step 8: Work 1 round of herringbone stitch with a 2-bead B inc between every column for a total of 16 beads (Figure 8). Step up.

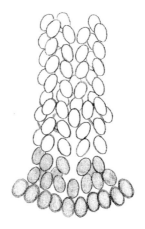

Figure 8

Step 9: Work 1 round of herringbone stitch for a total of 16 beads (Figure 9). Step up.

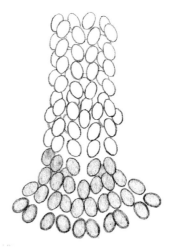

Figure 9

Step 10: *Work 1 herringbone stitch, a 1-bead B inc, and 1 herringbone stitch. Pass down through 2 and up through 2 (Figure 10).

Figure 10

Repeat from * 3 times. Step up. *Note:* See how the tube is now separated into four petals?

For clarity, from now on, I'm just going to show one of the four petals.

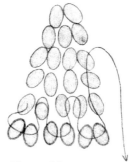

Figure 11

Step 11: *Work 1 herringbone stitch, a 2-bead B inc, and 1 herringbone stitch. Pass down through 3 and up through 3 (Figure 11). Repeat from * 3 times. Step up.

Step 12: *Work a 3-bead picot, a 1-bead B inc, a 5-bead picot, a 1-bead B inc, and a 3-bead picot. Pass down through 4 and up through 4 (Figure 12). Repeat from * 3 times. Run your thread up through the beads to the last pink row.

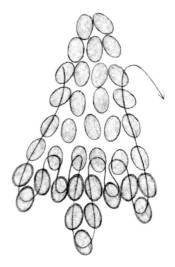

Figure 12

Outer Petals

Use all pink beads.

Step 13: Work 4 herringbone stitches on top of the last pink row (Figure 13). This forms the base for the outer petals. *Note:* You'll bead each outer petal separately. It's fiddly work, getting your needle into these tight spaces and keeping the tension snug while you turn, so be patient with yourself. Use the necessary turn (the ladder turn or Rita's turn), and keep the thread tension as tight as you can. Watch for thread catching around other petals.

Step 14: Work 1 row of herringbone stitch for a total of 2 beads (Figure 14).

Figure 14

Step 15: Work 1 row of 3 beads (a W inc) (Figure 15).

Figure 15

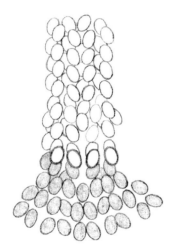

Figure 13

Step 16: Work 3 rows of herringbone stitch for a total of 4 beads in each row (Figure 16).

Step 17: Work 1 row of 1 herringbone stitch, a 1-bead B inc, and 1 herringbone stitch for a total of 5 beads (Figure 17).

Figure 17

Step 18: Work 1 row of 1 herringbone stitch, a 1-bead B dec, and 1 herringbone stitch for a total of 4 beads (Figure 18). Pull tight!

Figure 16

Figure 18

Step 19: Work 2 rows of herringbone stitch for a total of 4 beads in each row (Figure 19).

Step 20: Work 1 row of W dec for a total of 3 beads.

Step 21: Work 1 row of W dec for a total of 2 beads (Figure 20).

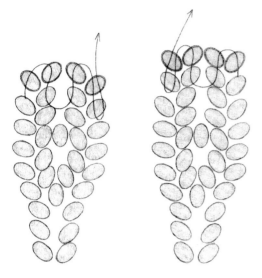

Figure 19

Figure 20

Figure 21

Step 22: Work one 3-bead picot (Figure 21). Make sure the petal is curling in the direction you want, then run your thread down through the petal-edge and flower beads to come out the next herringbone on top of another.

Step 23: Make 3 more petals the same way. Run your thread up through the flower to come out the top edge (your very first row).

CALYX

Use all green beads.

Step 24: Add a 1-bead picot to each herringbone stitch at the top edge for a total of 4 beads (Figure 22).

Step 25: Step up, then add 1 green bead between each "up" bead for a total of 4 beads (Figure 23). Step up. (Now you're

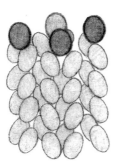

Figure 22

Figure 23

doing tubular peyote stitch—like how I snuck that in?)

Step 26: Work 4 more rounds of even-count tubular peyote stitch (4 beads in each round). Remember to step up on each row.

Step 27: Add a 6-bead loop to 2 opposite "up" beads. Pass through the beads again to reinforce the loop (Figure 24).

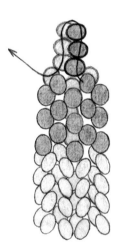

Figure 24

Step 28: Sew the remaining 2 "up" beads together underneath the loop. Drop your needle down through the center of the flower.

STAMENS

Step 29: String 3 pink, 3 bugles, 1 pink, 1 yellow, and 1 pink. Pass back up through the bugles and the 3 pinks to come out the top of the flower. (This is called double-run fringe.) Run your thread through the loop, pass the needle through the center, and make 3 more stamens in the same way. You can vary the number of bugles and seeds to make each one a different length. Pass through the hanging loop each time to re-inforce.

Step 30: Finish by tying off your thread and adding ear wires. Or you can string the fuchsias on the end of a lariat. Make a few leaves with the violet-leaf pattern on page 68 to add to the lariat, if you like.

GALLERY

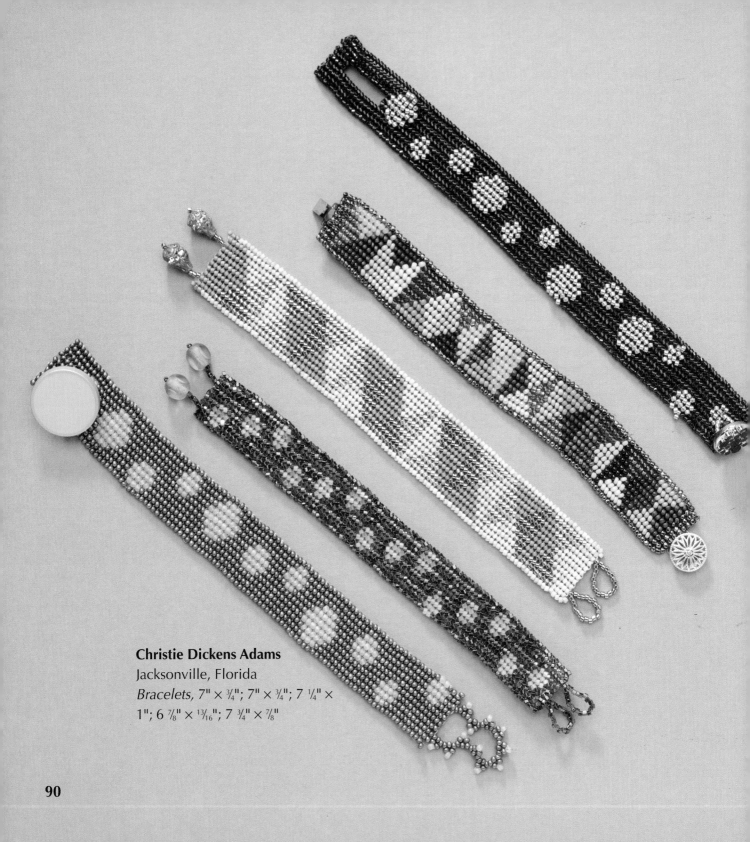

Christie Dickens Adams
Jacksonville, Florida
Bracelets, 7" × ¾"; 7" × ¾"; 7 ¼" × 1"; 6 ⅞" × ¹³⁄₁₆"; 7 ¾" × ⅞"

Anita Barniville
Fort Saint Lucie, Florida
Fuchsia Bracelet, 6⁵⁄₁₆" × 1⁷⁄₈" × 1"

Spring Bishop
Halfway, Oregon
Pendant, 5½" × 1¾"

Virginia Blakelock
Wilsonville, Oregon
Ndebele Sash, 3" × 4½'

Jane Davis
Ventura, California
Two Gate Purses,
11" × 3" × 3"; 11" × 2½" × 2½"

Isabee Thiebaut Demski
Reed City, Michigan
Amulet Bags, 12" × 2" × ³⁄₁₆";
12½" × 1¾" × ¼"

95

Wendy Ellsworth
Quakertown, Pennsyvania
Summer Passion, 20" × 3½" × 1½"

Roxa Scepter, 19" × 2" × 3"

Teyuk Semangka, 5" × 6¼" × 4½"

Suzanne Golden
New York, New York
Bracelet (produced in a class by
Sue Jackson and Wendy Hubrick
of Hummingbird Beads),
$8\frac{1}{4}" \times 1\frac{1}{16}" \times \frac{3}{8}"$

Barbara L. Grainger
Oregon City, Oregon
Tic-Tac-Toe Set, Board : $\frac{5}{16}" \times 5\frac{1}{2}"$;
Pieces: $1\frac{3}{4}" \times 1\frac{3}{4}" \times \frac{3}{4}"$

Dulcey Heller
St. Louis Park, Minnesota
Book Cover, 4¾" × 3" × ½"

Roni Hennen
Guerneville, California
Wizard Tapestry, 10½" × 7"

Abstract Tapestry, 18½" × 7"

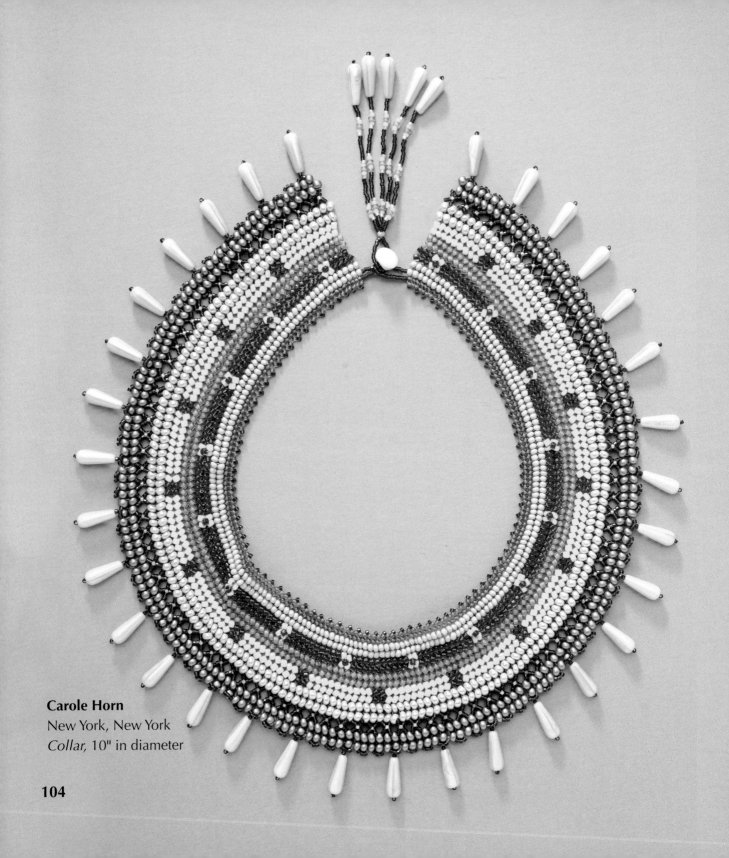

Carole Horn
New York, New York
Collar, 10" in diameter

Laurel Kubby
Phoenix, Arizona
Beaded Beads, between ⅜" and 1⁷⁄₁₆" × ½" and 2³⁄₁₆"

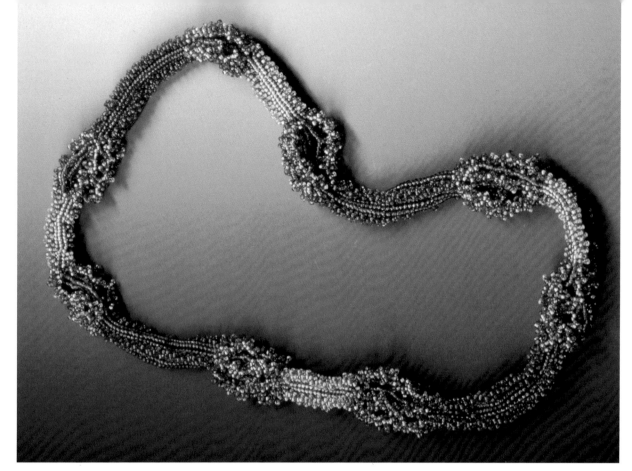

Haley Licata
Highland Park, Illinois
Necklace, 26½" × ½" × 1"

Alysse Manning
Castro Valley, California
Beaded Figurine, 4¾" × 2½" × 2½"

Donna Palmer
San Diego, California
Checkerboard Necklace, 6" diameter

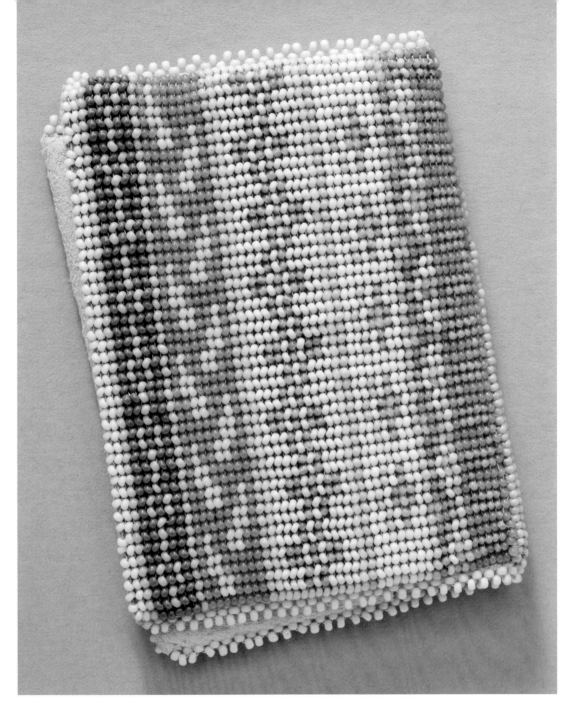

Carol Perrenoud
Wilsonville, Oregon
Fair Isle Card Holder, 6¼" × 4³⁄₁₆"

Wynter Rayne
Beaverton, Oregon
Bracelets, 7½" × 1¼"; 7½" × 1⁹⁄₁₆"; 6¼" × 1½"

Ann Severine
Solana Beach, California
Old Glass Reborn, 3" × 3½" × 1¼"

Fran Stone
Portland, Oregon
Choker, approximately
6" in diameter

112

Herringbone Czech bead graph

May be reproduced for personal use only.

Herringbone Delica bead graph

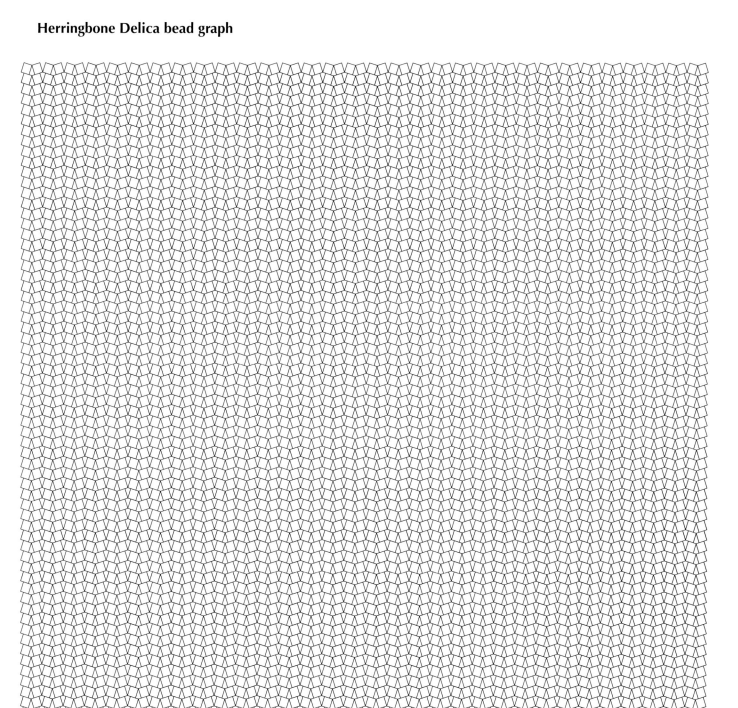

BIBLIOGRAPHY

Bead Society of Great Britain. *Newsletter.* Numbers 48, 56, and 59.

Blakelock, Virginia. *Those Bad, Bad Beads,* Sixth Edition. Wilsonville, Oregon: Self published, 1990.

Clark, Margaret Courtney. *Ndebele: Art of an African Tribe.* New York: Rizzoli, 1986.

Cook, Jeannette, and Vicki Star. *Beady Eyed Women's Guide to Exquisite Beadwork: An Off-Loom Bead Weaving Primer.* Encinitas, California: Self published, 1996.

Elbe, Barbara E. *Back to Beadin'.* Redding, Calfornia: B. E. E. Publishing, 1996.

Durant, Judith, and Jean Campbell. *The Beader's Companion.* Loveland, Colorado: Interweave Press, 1998.

July, Robert W. *A History of the African People.* New York: Charles Scribner's Sons, 1970.

Morris, Jean, and Eleanor Preston-Whyte. *Speaking with Beads: Zulu Arts from Southern Africa.* London: Thames and Hudson, 1994.

Stalcup, Ann. *Ndebele Beadwork: African Artistry (Crafts of the World).* Logan, Iowa: Powerkids Press, 1999.

SOURCES

BEADS, BOOKS, KITS, PATTERNS

Beadcats
PO Box 2840
Wilsonville, OR 97070-2840
(503) 625-2323
www.beadcats.com

Beady Eyed Women
Vicki Star and Jeannette Cook
PO Box 231093
Encinitas, CA 92023-1093
(760) 633-1247
(760) 633-1225 (fax)
www.beadyeyedwomen.com
vstar3@aol.com

Beyond Beadery
PO Box 460
Rollinsville, CO 80474
(303) 258-9389
(303) 258-9394 fax
www.beyondbeadery.com

Kandra's Gallery & Beads
570 Higuera St., Ste.125
San Luis Obispo, CA 93401
(800) 454-7079
(805) 544-7306
www.kandrasbeads.com

TASSEL STANDS

Judy Walker
PO Box 17924
Irvine, CA 92623
judywalker@pobox.com

BEAD BOOK AND MAGAZINE PUBLISHER

Interweave Press
201 East Fourth Street
Loveland, CO 80537-5655
(800) 272-2193
www.interweave.com

INDEX

SUBSCRIBE TO BEADWORK

Beadwork magazine is devoted to beadcrafting of all kinds. It's filled with fun-to-make projects in every technique you can think of—seed bead loomwork, peyote stitch, wirework, bead knitting and crochet, and more. You'll find gallery-quality work, artist profiles, tips, techniques, a calendar of bead events, and book and product reviews.

Six times a year, Beadwork—with its beautiful photographs and clear illustrations—brings you a whole world of up-to-the-minute bead buzz.

I year (6 issues) $24.95

CALL TODAY TO SUBSCRIBE
(800) 340-7496

EACH BOOK FOCUSES ON A SINGLE TECHNIQUE!

The **Beadwork How-To Books** combine projects, techniques, and a stunning gallery of contemporary beaded pieces into a beautifully illustrated, colorful format. The projects will open the door to the rich cultural history behind these techniques. Step by step you'll learn to create beaded tassels, necklaces, earrings, bracelets, amulets, vessels, pins, and other accessories that you have admired from afar.

8½ × 9, paperbound, 128 pages.
ISBN: 1-883010-63-2 — $21.95

8½ × 9, paperbound, 112 pages.
ISBN: 1-883010-71-3 — $21.95

LOOK
FOR INTERWEAVE books at your book or bead store, or call **(800) 272-2193.** Visit us online at **www.interweave.com.**

8½ × 9, paperbound, 128 pages
ISBN: 1-883010-72-1 — $21.95

8½ × 9, paperbound, 112 pages.
ISBN: 1-883010-73-X — $21.95

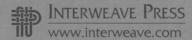

INTERWEAVE PRESS
www.interweave.com